Child of Wonder

Marty Haugen

Illustrated by Stephen Nesser

G-9398
ISBN: 978-1-62277-285-8

Copyright © 2018 GIA Publications, Inc.
7404 S. Mason Ave., Chicago, IL 60638 • www.giamusic.com
This book was printed in January 2018 by RR Donnelley in Shenzhen, China.

For _____

our child of wonder

From _____

INTRODUCTION

Child of Wonder was written to be sung at the baptism of Joshua Spitzack, the godson of my wife, Linda, and me. I wrote most of it in the car while Linda was driving us to the baptism. The song was originally intended to be sung as a solo after the actual baptism. However, for a number of years the congregation of our own faith community, Mayflower UCC, has sung it together as a newly-baptized child is carried through their midst.

While the lyrics of *Child of Wonder* celebrate the sacredness of human life and delight in the lives of children, they do not specifically articulate a Christian theology of baptism. For that reason, I was delighted that Stephen Nesser created artwork that celebrate birth rituals in a variety of religious faith traditions and cultures. While baptism is of course a common sacrament for most Christian denominations, rituals around the birth of a child are almost universal in human societies. I believe Stephen has done a beautiful job in researching and lovingly expressing many of those traditions.

I hope this book can help to bring joy and delight to children and to those who love and nurture them.

—Marty Haugen

For Quinn, Damian, William and Everett
—Marty

For Hannah, my child of wonder
—Stephen

Child of wonder, child of grace.
Love comes dancing 'round your face.

Child of water, child of earth

Gentle flower come to birth.

You shall be God's joyful singer.
You shall be life's joyous song.
Child of evening, child of night.

Child of morning, child of light.
Bring the daybreak and the sun.

God's own peace when day is done.
You shall be God's joyful dancer,
dance the moon and stars to sleep.

Child of dreams and our tomorrows
come to share our joys and sorrows
Child so helpless and so weak.

Such a power still you speak.

You shall be life's loving promise.

Hope of life amid our doubts.

You shall be God's joyful prophet.
Voice of life's resounding shout.

You shall be God's loving promise.
Let your song be lifted high.

You shall be God's joyful dancer.

Dance our joy across the sky.

Child of Wonder

Marty Haugen

1. Child of won - der, child of grace, love comes dan - cing 'round your face; Child of wat - er, child of earth, gen - tle flow - er come to birth.

2. Child of eve - ning, child of night, child of morn - ing, child of light; Bring the day - break and the sun, God's own peace when day is done.

3. Child of dreams and our to - mor - rows, come to share our joys and sor - rows; Child so help - less and so weak, such a pow - er still you speak.

You shall be God's joy-ful sing-er, you shall be life's joy-ous
You shall be God's joy-ful dan-cer, dance the moon and stars to
You shall be God's lov-ing prom-ise,
You shall be God's joy-ful sing-er,

song. hope of life a - mid our doubts;
sleep. let your song be lift - ed high;

You shall be God's joy-ful proph-et, voice of life's re - sound-ing
You shall be God's joy-ful danc-er, dance our joy a - cross the

To instrumental verse

shout. sky.

To instrumental verse

Child of wonder, child of grace...

These parents asked a man and woman, usually someone close to the family, to be the baby's padrinos (godparents). The padrinos will form a life-long intimate bond with the child. During the baptism, this family and minister pray for the child, and holy water is poured over the baby's forehead as was done by John the Baptist.

Gentle flower come to birth...

The Lama has drawn a mandala on the floor. The baby is blessed and his name is spoken by the Lama as he holds the baby over the mandala.

Child of morning, child of light...

This African family invited family and friends to join them at sunrise, where the father takes the child outside to see its first sunrise and announces the baby's name to the world.

Child of dreams and our tomorrows...

These Korean parents fly a Korean kite after the baby's birth. The high-flown kite predicts the child will live a peaceful and happy life.

You shall be life's loving promise...

These parents light a baptismal candle to guide the child in her journey of faith.

You shall be life's loving promise...

This Hindu family holds a namakaran (naming ceremony). The Hindu priest chants mantras praying for the baby's health. The father writes the baby's name in a plate of rice, touches the baby's lips with honey to show how sweet life can be, and then covers the babies ear with a betel leaf and whispers its name for the first time.